THE TO...
OUR M...

THE TONGUE –
OUR MEASURE

□ □ □

SIMO RALEVIĆ

THE BANNER OF TRUTH TRUST

THE BANNER OF TRUTH TRUST
3 Murrayfield Road, Edinburgh EH12 6EL
PO Box 621, Carlisle, Pennsylvania 17013, USA

*

© *Simo Ralević 1987*
First published 1987
ISBN 0 85151 507 X

*

Typeset in 11/12pt Linotron Times
at The Spartan Press Ltd, Lymington, Hants
Reproduced, printed and bound in Great Britain by
Hazell Watson & Viney Limited
Member of BPCC plc
Aylesbury Bucks

Contents

		PAGE
	INTRODUCTION	5
1.	THE BRIDLED AND THE UNBRIDLED TONGUE	7
2.	THE WAYS A BRIDLED TONGUE WILL NOT GO	26
3.	A BRIDLE FOR THE TONGUE	47

[3]

Introduction

In the original Serbo-Croat introduction to this book Simo Ralević wrote:

'This is a message very much needed by churches today. That is to say it is not enough merely to come to church, read the Bible and observe certain outward forms of godliness. Formalism is something which God greatly detests. Reality is what interests God. That which God does always begins from the heart. He renews man's inward being. When God saves a man he begins the work of bringing him under the control of Jesus Christ by the Holy Spirit. Let us ask the Holy Spirit to teach us by means of these messages.'

There can be no doubt about the relevance of this book to all Christians at this time. Our tongues were given us to glorify God. Conversion should lead us to use our tongues for this end. Sad to say there are some professing Christians who seem to make no attempt to control their tongues. As this book points out, such a person has no valid claim to be a Christian at all.

Even where an attempt is made to exercise control of the tongue, great difficulties are encountered. This book should serve to encourage and instruct those who desire to be wholly subject to Scripture and really to live to God's glory. The tongue can be productive of much good. Let us pray that God will teach us throroughly in this area.

Simo Ralević is a Yugoslav minister who has laboured for many years in South-Eastern Yugoslavia. He uses to the full the opportunities the authorities in that land give for the preaching of the gospel and the building up of churches. He is known as a worthy defender of evangelical truth and as strongly opposing that which is superficial and false in religion. In a day of compromise and half-heartedness Simo Ralević is known among Christians all over Yugoslavia as wholeheartedly committed to the maintenance of reformed doctrine.

While best-known as a preacher he has also written a number of books in the Serbo-Croat and Macedonian languages and these are widely circulated and read with much benefit. It is good that we have the opportunity of publishing this first translation of one of his books into English.

The Publishers, June 1987

1

THE BRIDLED AND THE
UNBRIDLED TONGUE

If any man among you seem to be religious, and bridleth not his tongue, but deceiveth his own heart, this man's religion is vain.
(James 1: 26)

Often, when we go to the doctor's, the first thing he says is, 'Show me your tongue'! Of course, every good doctor knows how to diagnose by means of the tongue symptoms of illnesses which have arisen through what we have eaten. You can tell whether someone eats good or bad food by his tongue. The tongue is our identity card! And just as this is true from the physical point of view, so it is from the spiritual. You can tell from our speech with what food we are feeding our souls.

Brothers and sisters, I do not intend to speak to you now about the gift of tongues, but rather about the correct use of the tongue which God has given us.

The tongue is set in a most slippery place and can very easily slip up and cause great damage. A certain Greek philosopher used to start off his conversations with the words: 'Say something so that I can see you'. A great statement!

As the minister of this congregation I am bound to speak to you about this matter. And I wish to expound my theme to you in as detailed a manner as possible, so I shall work round it in three sermons. The basic text which I have selected is

James 1: 26: 'If any man among you seem* to be religious and bridleth not his tongue, but deceiveth his own heart, this man's religion is vain'. So the theme of all three sermons is: *A bridled tongue is a measure of right and true faith.*

I want to say a few words about the Epistle of James, so that we can see this text in a broad framework. James, who describes himself as 'a servant of the Lord Jesus Christ', had been taking pains to explain that faith which is in the head alone is not saving faith. He was writing to men and women professing Christ, some of whom had fallen into a certain form of great religious error. Some were deceiving themselves by thinking that it was enough to have a certain amount of knowledge and to fulfil certain rites, which are only an exterior form of godliness, in order to be saved. And James strikes ceaselessly at the root of this deception.

These people thought that it was enough to believe and to know that there is one God. James says: 'No! The devils also believe, and tremble'. James wishes to underline this. Certainly saving faith includes head knowledge; it has also its outward signs; but it consists of much more than these things! Thus he says, 'If any man among you seem to be religious and bridleth not his tongue, but deceiveth his own heart, this man's religion is vain'.

Let us go straight to an examination of the text.

1: The person whom James has in mind
Of whom was James thinking when he wrote about the tongue? The answer is clearly shown in

* or 'thinks himself' (NASB), 'Considers himself' (NIV).

his words, 'If any man among you seemeth to be religious'.

a. *It was someone who considered himself a believer*

James is thinking of anybody who fulfils certain conditions. 'If any man among you . . .' James is speaking generally, 'If any man'. Just as Paul, too, said, 'If any man be in Christ he is a new creature', even so James says: 'If any man among you seem to be religious'.

Clearly James is writing to those who think they are believers, those who have some sort of knowledge and who have performed certain duties. They had become 'believers' in Christ and were doing things which people who are saved must do. Obviously, therefore, they were men and women who had been coming regularly and punctually to services; they were men, women and children who had sung hymns in the house of prayer. They were even people who had taken part in prayer. So they were men, women and children who thought themselves to be believers, and who were thought by others to be believers.

Thus this text applies to everyone who comes to the house of prayer confessing faith, 'If *anyone* thinks himself to be religious'. And I hope you all see yourselves as believers. It would be very strange if somebody came to church without believing! Apart from belief, I do not know what other motives can bring people here.

Those who are not here today but rather are spending their time in front of the television set, reading newspapers, going for walks or playing football have every right to look upon themselves as non-believers, for believers are to be in the house of God on Sundays. And so we have noticed that James wrote these words to those who call themselves believers.

b. *His condition*

In what condition does the person of whom James speaks find himself? How does James describe his state? These are his words, 'and bridleth not his tongue, but deceiveth his own heart'. Thus it is a two-fold condition, an unbridled tongue and a deceived heart.

When he says 'and bridleth not his tongue' he means the organ of speech explicitly. We have in Serbo-Croat the expression 'she has a long tongue'. In so saying we do not imagine, literally, a long tongue, but rather one that does too much wagging. Or, as James puts it, an unbridled tongue. An unbridled tongue, or one that is given free rein, of course does not mean one of which the muscles have become loose so that it falls out of the mouth, but rather it means the abuse of the tongue.

The same word James also uses in chapter three verse two: 'For in many things we offend all. If any man offend not in word, the same is a perfect man, and able also to bridle the whole body'. The word 'to bridle' comes from the noun 'bridle'. And what are bridles used for? They are put in horses' mouths. By their help we can constantly control and direct them; they help to direct the powerful movements of the horse to maximum use. Such is the role of bridles. But as an unbridled horse running loose on a road may do great damage and waste its energy, James states that in the same way great damage is done by a tongue which is not bridled. The tongue needs to have a bridle which will direct all human energy towards good. An unbridled tongue is destructive wherever it appears.

Such, therefore, is the condition of the man of whom James is writing. But he now proceeds to speak of a second characteristic of the same person; he also 'deceiveth his own heart'. Of course, when he says 'the heart', James does not mean the physical organ which pumps blood. By the biblical term 'heart' the inner being is meant. The word includes our reason, our perception and our will. What I am at heart, that I am in essence.

James is obviously writing about people who think themselves believers, and whom others consider to be believers, but whose tongues are unbridled and who are deceived in their hearts. However, it is well said, 'but deceiveth his own heart'. This word 'but' suggests that a deceived heart and an unbridled tongue fit together like hand and glove. An unbridled tongue is a sure sign of a deceived heart.

How terrible it is, my dear friends, when a man goes to meetings, sings and prays, reads the Bible, and performs all the outward rituals, yet at the same time does not bridle his tongue! An unbridled tongue is a sure sign that such a man (or woman) is deceiving his own heart and comes short of possessing true saving faith.

c. *What sort of religion has this man?*

James supplies the answer to our question: 'this man's religion is vain'.

His knowledge of God and all his outward religious observances are self-deception. That sort of religion is vain, useless, empty; it is not substantial, saving religion. It is but straw. It is dead. It is a religion akin to the devil's. No matter what this person thinks of himself, no matter what others think of him, if he has an unbridled tongue, he has false religion. It is not I who says this, it is God through the mouth of James who says, 'this man's religion is vain'!

If this is so, and James says that it is, what principles can we draw from this conclusion, on which we shall be able to base our further study of the tongue?

d. *Some principles for further study*

These are the principles. The outward manifestation of true faith always flows from an inward reality. Outward works there must be, but God-pleasing, Christian duties cannot be separated from what is inward. James combines the two as he goes on to say in the next verse: 'Pure religion and undefiled before God and the Father is this, To visit the fatherless and widows in their affliction, and to keep himself unspotted from the world' (1: 27). It is in such ways that saving faith always manifests itself.

The extent to which saving faith has grasped our hearts is to be measured by the extent to which the Holy Spirit and the Word of God have disciplined and controlled our tongues. James states clearly that if there is no bridling of the tongue, neither is there saving faith. Anyone who has saving faith in his heart strives against sin in himself, and especially so against the sin of the tongue, for the Bible says, 'For sin shall not have dominion over you' (Romans 6: 14).

If we have saving faith, we shall also be interested in what the Bible teaches about this subject, and how we may possess a bridled tongue. And as a bridled tongue is a sign of true, saving faith, therefore I, and all present in my congregation today who are saved, will be interested to know what 'to have a bridled tongue' means. That is the motive for our investigation, to which we now come.

2: What does the Bible say about a bridled tongue?

Let us look briefly at some verses from both the Old and New Testaments.

a. *There is death and life in the power of the tongue*

Let us look first at Proverbs 18: 20, 21, where we read: 'A man's belly shall be satisfied with the fruit of his mouth; and with the increase of his lips shall he be filled. Death and life are in the power of the tongue: and they that love it shall eat the fruit thereof'.

The tongue has in its power both life and death. It has the power to bless or curse. The tongue has the power to bring down on a person God's wrath or God's blessing, for time and for eternity.

Solomon says, 'and they that love it shall eat the fruit thereof'. His words convey the same meaning as those of the apostle Paul who wrote, 'Whatsoever a man soweth, that shall he also reap'. What we sow with the tongue, the same will be the fruit yielded. If we sow with the tongue to the flesh, we shall reap death; if, however, we sow to the spirit we shall reap life everlasting. 'Death and life are in the power of the tongue'.

The words 'death and 'life' often recur in the Bible. They are found throughout the Old Testament in the messages which God spoke to Israel. 'Life' means knowing God and having communion with him. 'Death' means being dead to God and not having eternal life. Eternal death is linked with the Lake of Fire, eternal separation from God. Death and life proceed from the tongue.

Therefore, is it not a terrible weapon which can bring death when without a bridle, without control? An unbridled tongue is more dangerous than an atom bomb. Therefore, what a tragedy it is when a tongue which is to some extent unbridled is found in the life of a Christian!

b.   *God hates an unbridled tongue*

In Proverbs 6: 16–19 the LORD says: 'These six things doth the LORD hate: yea, seven are an abomination unto him: a proud look [proud eyes are an indication of a proud and haughty heart], a lying tongue, and hands that shed innocent blood, an heart that deviseth wicked imaginations, feet that be swift in running to mischief, a false witness that speaketh lies, and he that soweth discord among brethren'. God hates these seven things, and three of the evils mentioned in this text are linked with the activity of the tongue. Have you noticed that God places in the same category as murder 'a lying tongue', 'a false witness' and 'he that soweth discord among brethren'?

In Proverbs 8: 13 we find a verse parallel to those you have just heard: 'The fear of the LORD is to hate evil: pride and arrogancy, and the evil way, and the froward mouth do I hate'.

God's will for us is that we should be conformed

to the image of his Son. That is what the Bible says. Now, to be conformed to the likeness of Jesus Christ means to love what Jesus loves and to hate what Jesus hates. That is God's intention for us. Well now: what attitude has God towards lying lips? He hates them as much as he hates murder. In view of that, if we have been conformed to the likeness of Jesus Christ, we shall restrain our tongue by our knowledge of the Word of God and by the aid of the Holy Spirit.

God is a wrathful God, he hates an unbridled tongue.

c. *A bridled tongue is a path to blessing*
In Psalm 34: 11–13 we read: 'Come, ye children, hearken unto me: I will teach you the fear of the LORD. What man is he that desireth life, and loveth many days, that he may see good'? Come, then, children, let us listen to him, and you adults. Does anyone among you desire that his life should be full of bitterness and misfortune and that he should quickly die? Does any one of you, children, wish that you had a bad mother and father, who constantly quarrel and fight? Which of you wishes to die in the prime of life? Such is the questioning of the psalmist: 'What man is he that desireth life'? – This does not mean mere existence, but 'who is there among us who desires a righteous, godly life: communion with God'! He that desires this, 'loveth many days'. This means a long life filled with good. To those who desire this, the psalmist gives a recipe: 'Keep thy tongue from evil and thy lips from speaking guile'.

He who wants to lead a righteous life must have a bridled tongue.

Lest any of you should start thinking that this is only meant for Old Testament times, here is the teaching of the apostle Peter. In 1 Peter 3: 8–10 he gives us these words: 'Finally, be ye all of one mind, having compassion one of another, love as brethren, be pitiful, be courteous: not rendering evil for evil, or railing for railing: but contrariwise blessing; knowing that ye are thereunto called, that ye should inherit a blessing'. Why must we do this? Peter proceeds: 'For he that will love life, and see good days, let him refrain his tongue from evil, and his lips that they speak no guile'. So, you see, a bridled tongue brings blessings.

What is the reason why many do not experience the 'good days' promised, yet perhaps wonder why this should be? You experience spiritual aridity and trouble. Maybe the cause is just this. Maybe it is the Lord's chastening hand for an insufficiently bridled tongue.

I am not saying that if you have misfortune in your life this must be due to an unbridled tongue. Troubles can come for other reasons. However, if we do not live our days with the Lord, it could well be because we do not refrain our tongue from evil.

d. *The use of the tongue is an automatic, outward indication of the inward spiritual development of a child of God*

This is what James means when he says: 'For in many things we offend all. If any man offend not in word, the same is a perfect man, and able also to bridle the whole body' (3: 2). The man who is enabled to bridle his tongue is also fitted to direct his whole life according to God's will.

That is the truth! How developed are we,

spiritually? How can we measure someone's inward, spiritual development? The tongue is an automatic, outward indication of the spiritual development of a child of God.

Some of us have learned much from the Bible. We listen to sermons, we read books, we are regular attenders at services. All of this is excellent and commendable, but it is not enough. James says that a better proof of spiritual development is a bridled tongue. Are we bridling our tongue, restraining it from speaking the things which we once did? Is the Lord Jesus Christ holding the reins to our tongue? Is our tongue speaking that which the Lord wishes?

e. *By the misuse of the tongue we grieve the Holy Spirit*

In Ephesians 4: 25–30 the apostle Paul writes: 'Wherefore putting away lying, speak every man truth with his neighbour: for we are members one of another. Be ye angry, and sin not: Let not the sun go down upon your wrath: Neither give place to the devil. Let him that stole steal no more: but rather let him labour, working with his hands the thing which is good, that he may have to give to him that needeth. Let no corrupt communication proceed out of your mouth, but that which is good to the use of edifying, that it may minister grace unto the hearers. And grieve not the holy Spirit of God, whereby ye are sealed unto the day of redemption'.

These verses bear clear witness to us that the misuse of the tongue is an outward sign of grieving the Holy Spirit. Inward grieving of the Spirit is provoked by 'all bitterness, and wrath, and anger . . .'. But an outward grievance is the work of the unbridled tongue. And when we grieve him, the Holy Spirit curtails his work in us.

It could be for just this reason that some people are not progressing in their spiritual lives. The Holy Spirit will not work among us and within us if we do not bridle our tongue.

Parallel verses to those I have just given you are found in Ephesians 5: 18 and onwards: 'And be not drunk with wine, wherein is excess; but be filled with the Spirit', and Paul goes on to cite five things that indicate a life filled with the Spirit. He says: '*Speaking* to yourselves in psalms and hymns and spiritual songs, *singing* and *making melody* in your heart to the Lord; *giving thanks* always . . . *submitting yourselves* one to another in the fear of God'. And four out of these five things are linked to the tongue.

But this principle, spirituality, which has to do with fulness of the Spirit, is proportionate to how much the Holy Spirit uses a man's tongue towards good fellowship and to God's glory.

A bridled tongue, a tongue which expresses itself to the benefit of the congregation, is one of the signs of a man who has the fulness of the Spirit.

f. *The tongue will either justify us at the Day of Judgment, or condemn us*

In the twelfth chapter of Matthew's Gospel we read that our Lord Jesus had discourse with the Pharisees. They ascribed his miracles to Satan, and the Lord Jesus warned them about blasphemy against the Holy Spirit. And then he continues: 'O generation of vipers, how can ye, being evil, speak good things? for out of the abundance of the heart the mouth speaketh. A good man out of the good treasure of the heart bringeth forth good things: and an evil man out of the evil treasure bringeth forth evil things. But I say unto you, That every idle word that men shall speak, they shall give account thereof in the day of judgment. For by thy words thou shalt be justified, and by thy words thou shalt be condemned'. (12: 34–37).

Jesus began by speaking to the Pharisees, and then extended his message to the general public: 'Every idle word that *men* shall speak . . .'. He means everyone here, including you and me. The Lord says that we shall justify or condemn ourselves by our words. We know that justification is by faith, not by works. But Jesus is speaking of a quite different justification here, justification at the Judgment. According to this, our words will reveal on Judgment Day whether or not we are converted!

How vital it is, therefore, to have a bridled tongue! This is what the words of Christ testify to us: 'For by thy words thou shalt be justified and by thy words thou shalt be condemned'. That stands to reason, because the tongue is the vent of our heart. The use of our tongue alone will be a sufficient indication, a sufficient proof of the righteousness of God in our condemnation, or else an evidence of our salvation.

So James is perfectly right when he says: 'If any man among you seem to be religious, and bridleth not his tongue, but deceiveth his own heart, this man's religion is vain'.

Of the Lord Jesus the apostle Peter writes: 'Who did no sin, neither was guile found in his mouth' (1 Peter 2: 22). If we are saved we are in process of being conformed to the image of Jesus

Christ, and therefore to a certain extent these words should be true of us: 'neither was guile found in his mouth'.

Let us look to the Lord. Let us beseech his aid.

3: False witness and corrupt communication

Next we shall take a brief look at some paths along which a bridled tongue does not walk, namely, false witness, and filthy speech.

a. *False Witness*

The ninth of the Ten Commandments reads: 'Thou shalt not bear false witness against thy neighbour' (Exodus 20: 16). Which sins are included in this commandment? It is hard even to number them. Nevertheless, let us make an attempt. They include all the casting of doubt upon the truth, the staining of our name and other people's names. They include perjury in particular, the telling of lies in order that we may support that which is evil, the calling evil good and good evil, the justifying of wickedness and the labelling as wickedness that which is good and true. Acquiescing in the conceal-ment of the truth is a further evidence of perjury. And even when we do speak the truth we may sin – perhaps by speaking at the wrong time and for the wrong motive, or by presenting it in an ambiguous or misleading manner. We break the command-ment also by gossiping, slandering, whispering, promoting false rumours, and using abusive lan-guage. The incorrect presentation of facts and deliberate twisting of certain words, flattery and vainglorious boasting; the speaking about oneself or others in a exaggerated way, or with seemingly humble obsequiousness wrapped in pride, saying for example, 'your least brother' – all these are evil. The exaggeration of mistakes or the covering up of sin, the unnecessary revelation of others' weaknesses, the acceptance of false accusations and the failure to defend the person you know to be innocent, yet wrongfully accused, – these, too, are sins. To rejoice at somebody's downfall, to fail to fulfil promises, are also evil. All of these and many more are the sins enumerated as being under prohibition in the ninth commandment. They belong to the way in which a bridled tongue will not go. If we were to look at this commandment in close detail we would need months in which to do it. The same commandment is repeated in Deuteronomy 5: 20. Thomas Watson says of this commandment: 'God has set two natural fences to keep in the tongue – the teeth and the lips; and this commandment is a third fence set about it, "Neither shalt thou bear false witness against thy neighbour".'

The commandments on the second table of the Law reveal God's will to preserve the sanctity of human life, the sanctity of family and married life, the sanctity of private property, and the sanctity of a man's good name. 'Thou shalt not kill' reveals the sanctity of life. 'Honour thy father and thy mother', 'Thou shalt not commit adultery' – here is the sanctity of family and married life. 'Thou shalt not steal' – here, with great brevity, is revealed the sanctity of our neighbour's private property. In the commandment: 'Thou shalt not bear false witness against thy neighbour' is contained the sanctity of a man's good name.

We must not bear false witness, not produce

false information. The apostle Paul also repeats this in the Epistle to the Ephesians 4: 25: 'Wherefore, putting aside lying, speak every man truth with his neighbour: for we are members one of another'.

One of the distinguishing features of God's people is that they do not lie. Whosoever continues in a way of conscious lying has every reason to doubt his faith. In Revelation 21: 8 the Lord says: '. . . all liars, shall have their part in the lake which burneth with fire and brimstone which is the second death'. Of the heavenly Jerusalem he writes: 'And there shall in no wise enter into it any thing that defileth, neither whatsoever worketh abomination, or maketh a lie'.

Lying is a sin present in children. In order to conceal one sin, they lie and thus commit another, so that their parents might not beat them. But they do not think of the Lake of Fire.

And not only are we forbidden from thinking up lies, we also must not present or spread the lies of others. 'Thou shalt not raise a false report', reads Exodus 23: 1, 'put not thine hand with the wicked to be an unrighteous witness'. But how slow we are to obey these laws fully! That is why throughout the whole Bible we read that it is forbidden to condemn an accused person on the testimony of a single witness. Always the Bible demands two or three witnesses. This is to prevent our believing false accusations.

A certain brother, a single man, was seen with a girl walking arm-in-arm, and it was broadcast that he was not living respectably. It later transpired that this girl was his sister. It is plain to see that in attempting to judge another's motives, we may easily judge amiss. If evil rumours about a person are filling the air, we must pay no heed to them unless there is solid evidence of truth, backed by honest witnesses.

A bridled tongue does not lie, and it does not gossip. The man who lies and gossips carries the devil about in his heart and tongue, and the man who listens receives the devil into his ears. Who are those men and women who sit within God's bower and on his holy hill? Psalm 15: 2, 3 says: 'He that walketh uprightly and worketh righteousness, and speaketh the truth in his heart; he that back-biteth not with his tongue, nor doeth evil to his neighbour, nor taketh up a reproach against his neighbour'.

b. *Corrupt communication*

A bridled tongue does not go the way of transgression against the ninth commandment. In the same way a bridled tongue does not walk the way of corrupt speaking. In Ephesians 4: 29, Paul says: 'Let no corrupt communication proceed out of your mouth, but that which is good' unto the hearers.

This word 'corrupt' originates in something putrid. Let me explain. It is as when we speak of perished fruit, rotten flesh, spoiled and repulsive garden produce, mouldy bread which is not fit to eat. Rotten food, if you eat it, can produce pain and death. Yet food serves to give strength and health to an organism. The same thing applies to spiritual health as well. For spiritual health, healthy thoughts and sound words are important. 'Let no corrupt communication proceed out of your mouth'.

Our words show with what we are feeding our minds: 'for out of the abundance of the heart the mouth speaketh'. This is why the apostle instructs us that corrupt communication must not proceed out of our mouths into the ears of our neighbours. Why is this? Because it hinders faith. And Paul further says that our speech must be 'that which is good to the use of edifying, that it may minister grace unto the hearers'.

Foul words and jokes are hostile to faith and do not minister grace; rather they destroy faith and poison spiritual health. This is why Paul proceeds to warn the Ephesians in chapter 5, verse 4 'Neither filthiness, nor foolish talking, nor jesting, which are not convenient'. Instead he urges the 'giving of thanks'.

Decent, relevant and instructive jokes may have their uses, but I have noticed that when spiritual brethren begin to relate fitting, edifying, humorous anecdotes, then unspiritual, immature believers start up with tales which are out of place and even disgraceful. The apostle Paul cautions us that this is destructive. It is not the way of a bridled tongue.

Is it not the case that when someone speaks disparagingly about a fellow believer, and we hear it, then our relationship with our brother or sister is liable to change instantly. Evil communications, unloving words, break up our brotherhood and smash up our fellowship.

But this command, as every other, teaches us not only what we must not do, but also what we have a vested interest in doing: 'Let no corrupt communication proceed out of your mouth but that which is good to the use of edifying, that it may minister grace to the hearers'. Do you love the congregation of Christ? Then do not be the authors of lies and unkind words. Do not listen when anyone relates to you anything other than that which is good, and only good.

How right James was when he wrote: 'If any man among you seem to be religious, and bridleth not his tongue, but deceiveth his own heart, this man's religion is vain'. Oh! how we must cry to God like the psalmist in Psalm 39: 1, 'I said, I will take heed to my ways, that I sin not with my tongue: I will keep my mouth with a bridle, while the wicked is before me'.

On the fearful Day of Judgment it will be enough to condemn us if we have broken the ninth commandment alone. But let it be remembered that to take heed lest one sin with one's tongue, and to set a bridle on one's mouth, is impossible for a man trusting in his own strength. For this it is needful that he be born again. The Lord Jesus died in sinners' place for their transgression of all commandments. Let us turn to him for forgiveness and cleansing in his blood, and for the strength to bridle our tongues.

Let us begin today to amend our speech. May we not be as the man of whom James says: 'For he beholdeth himself, and goeth his way, and straightway forgetteth what manner of man he was' (1: 24).

May the Lord have mercy on us and work in us so that we become conformed to the image of our Lord Jesus Christ, even in respect of our tongue and its use. Amen.

2

THE WAYS A BRIDLED TONGUE
WILL NOT GO

If any man among you seem to be religious, and bridleth not his tongue, but deceiveth his own heart, this man's religion is vain. (James 1: 26).

We have seen that a bridled tongue is a sign of the possession of true faith. It is a measure of the condition of our faith. James is an apostle of practical theology, who expounds the distinguishing features of true, saving faith. One of those distinguishing marks is a man's speech. According to the extent to which our tongue is bridled, the authenticity of our faith can be seen. But whoever thinks himself a believer and does not bridle his tongue has futile religion.

In verse 22 the apostle writes: 'But be ye doers of the word, and not hearers only, deceiving your own selves'. Whoever only hears God's word, and does not fulfil it, the same is deceived. Whoever thinks himself a believer, and does not have a bridle on his tongue, is obviously deceiving himself, deceiving his own heart as James says, and his is a hypocritical and false religion.

The Bible devotes a significant amount of space to this matter in both the Old and New Testaments. But we cannot expound it exhaustively, for then we would need to speak for months on end. But it is very important that I should speak God's Word to you concerning it, because our faith is only as authentic as our tongue is bridled. I repeat that the tongue is a measure of the authenticity of our faith. And our faith, in point of fact, is not some abstract thing. On the contrary, it is intensely practical and must be seen at work in our daily lives.

In our previous sermon we established that a bridled tongue does not bear false witness, nor transmit false information and slander about others. In this manner it does not engage in corrupt communication. Today I wish to describe some further ways in which a bridled tongue will not go. It does not go the way of disgraceful speech or unpermitted speech.

1: The misuse of the tongue

It is written in Colossians 3: 8, 'But now ye also put off all these; anger, wrath, malice, blasphemy, filthy communication out of your mouth'. Whoever speaks filthily misuses his tongue.

a. *Disgraceful language – abusive language*

Disgraceful language, which is so frequently heard nowadays, proceeds from a rotten heart and unclean thoughts. In his Epistle to the Ephesians Paul writes: 'it is a shame even to speak of those things which are done of them in secret' (5: 12).

For some men and women the chief topic of conversation concerns the shameful things which the godless do in secret. Immoral conversations and jokes are widespread today. Paul assures us that such abuse of the tongue is not fitting for saints. 'But now, you too throw off all this: anger, wrath, malice and blasphemy, shameful words

[27]

from your mouths'*.

Dr Čarnić has translated 'shameful words' as 'abusive language'. I think that his translation is better than that in the English Authorised Version because it is more all-embracing. Shameful words are included within abusive language. And if someone has anger, wrath, malice and blasphemy in his heart, it will manifest itself in abusive language.

Brothers and sisters, I take no delight in speaking about sin. I would be much happier speaking about the person and work of our Lord Jesus Christ, or about the new heavens and the new earth. When I describe sin, I am describing and examining myself also, and that is painful. But if we wish to be faithful to God's Word, then we must speak about sin in its various aspects.

Disgraceful language is a scourge, a very coarse whip which leaves deep, unhealing wounds. The tongue was created in order to produce life, and minister grace unto the hearers, to the building up of their faith. Unfortunately many use it as a fatal weapon.

When a man loses his temper or feels himself let down by someone else, the weapon which is nearest at hand to defend himself, or to launch an attack, is the tongue. If someone is jealous of another, he uses the tongue in place of a machine gun and slays him with words of abuse. And we use our tongue very frequently as a defensive weapon. Then we scarcely weigh our words; the ruder the

*Here the scripture (Colossians 3: 8) is given as a literal re-translation from the Serbian, in order not to obscure Simo Ralević's next comment.

better! The tongue becomes a veritable fire. Like a dragon it pours out death-bringing flames.

b. *Rebuking in love*

Perhaps someone might be saying now, 'Hey, brother Simo, did you not tell us that if a brother sins, we must rebuke him and not tolerate sin in him'? Yes, that is true, and I have not forgotten about it. There is such a thing as rebuke to those who are out of order, which is beneficial to spiritual health. The Bible says, 'Open rebuke is better than secret love' (Proverbs 27: 5). However, this sort of use of the tongue is a very different thing from disgraceful, abusive language used in aggression or self-defence!

For, beloved in the Lord, when I rebuke my brother or my neighbour, I do it always in love. I seek his benefit. But he who uses abusive language is seeking to avenge himself and to destroy his brother. When I rebuke my brother, I do so because the Bible teaches me so, and then I keep any vengefulness or abusiveness in me under control. But when somebody makes an attack, or defends his ego abusively, he is not keeping to biblical principles.

Observe this well. When I perceive that my brother is sinning against himself, against God, or against me, and I have to reproach him, then my feelings are often such that either I will attack him, or just let him alone. Yet the divine nature and biblical principles teach me that, if I love him, then I must both rebuke and at the same time help him. When I rebuke my brother, my motivation is always to be love to my brother, desire to win him, and not to lose him. But when a man uses abusive language, he does not show himself minded to win his brother, but to break him and kill him with words.

Today we are speaking against the sort of speech which has as its objective not to help, but to destroy.

c. *How does abusive language express itself?*

How does this abusive language express itself in family relationships? Paul says: 'But now ye also put off all these; anger, wrath, malice, blasphemy, filthy communication out of your mouth'. But it is extremely regrettable that in many Christian homes shameful, abusive language is to be heard between husband and wife.

The relationship between husband and wife, according to the Bible, must be as a visible relationship of Christ and the church, yet it is often like the relationship of Satan and the church, since Satan is the accuser of the brethren. Sometimes a husband feels disillusioned with his wife. And what can the wife do? One who is physically stronger than her husband may know how to crush him, but many cannot do this, and so they use their tongues as a whip – for the husband's back! If it were possible to peer into the heart of many a wife, the back of her husband would be seen there, livid all over from the stripes.

But the condition of the heart of many a husband is no better. It goes without saying that husbands should rebuke their wives in love, as Christ does his church. However, many husbands are in the habit not only of hitting their wives, but doing far worse, and much more demeaning than that: they completely beat them up with their tongues.

[30]

Whoever wishes to collaborate with Satan in guiding his children to the road to hell need only use foul language in the house. And if that is what happens, as I am afraid it does, then repentance – in front of the children – must also happen. And what sort of relationship is to exist between parents and children? When children are disobedient what do we say to them? Do we speak insultingly to them, saying for instance, 'You idiot'! or things like that? If so, we may cut wounds into their hearts which they then carry all their lives.

There are many men, women and children who have been undone to such an extent by such scourging of the tongue that they are socially crippled for life. I know a case where a wife was for ever saying to her husband that he was nothing, that he could not do anything, and in the end she actually produced in him an inferiority complex, so that now he dare not do anything. Such people go through life maladjusted because of abusive strictures.

And what is the relationship of children to their parents? The parents make a rule which the children must obey, but they do not like it. They cannot beat their mother and father, so what do they do? Within their own hearts, they abuse their father and mother! And when they are in the company of other children they say that their parents are stupid and old-fashioned. How insulting it is that, when parents require obedience, then their children make excuses or answer back to the contrary!

Abusive language is in evidence today even in church relationships. Some church members are constantly seeking to draw attention to themselves, and if things do not work out as they please, then they start 'telling tales' and asserting there is no love between believers. And regrettably some of the offenders are believers who still, year by year, are supposed to be teachers in the church. It is exceedingly dangerous when opposed groups start to form within a church. Any conspiracy behind people's backs is satanic.

Abusive language manifests itself nowadays in nervous car drivers. If somebody obstructs another's path or makes some sort of mistake, say, by turning without signalling, then instantly the driver or whoever is in the passenger seat will utter some word of abuse.

Do you see how practical James is being when he says: 'If any man among you seem to be religious, and bridleth not his tongue, but deceiveth his own heart, this man's religion is vain.'?

Neither must abusive language express itself in industry between workers and bosses. Sometimes it is required that you should work after normal working hours; sometimes pay is not on time. Various difficulties may arise. On such occasions the Christian must not use abusive words. The same applies in school as between teacher and pupil.

And I will say one more thing. As citizens of our state we must not speak abusively about anyone in power, rather we should pray for them.

d. *What was the attitude of the Lord Jesus Christ towards evil speech?*

In Matthew 5: 21, 22 we read these words: 'Ye have heard that it was said by them of old time, Thou shalt not kill; and whosoever shall kill shall be in danger of the judgment: But I say unto you, that whosoever is angry with his brother without a cause shall be in danger of the judgment: and whosoever shall say to his brother, Raca, shall be in danger of the council: but whosoever shall say, Thou fool, shall be in danger of hell fire'. What does the Lord Jesus teach us by these words? If one person says to another, 'you imbecile', 'you fool', 'you idiot', or some similar word, the indication is that such a man is a brigand and a murderer in his soul, and that he has a spirit of bloodshed within him.

Murder is the deliberate taking by a man of the life of another and this is contrary to God's law. And hatred, when it is in the world, often manifests itself in murder. Hatred, and also abusive language, is murder at root. The Jews of old held that murder was committed when a human life was taken by another. But our Lord informs us that whoever detests another person or speaks abusively about another, commits murder in his heart. Men look at what is before their eyes, but the Lord looks at the heart.

The murderer, taking up a rifle or a pistol, shoots and kills. The denunciator takes up abusive words, murderous words, and creates from them bullets; you cannot see when they hit, yet they cause many wounds, greater and more dangerous than we might imagine. Therefore, my dear friends, when such a spirit is manifested in ourselves, we must be merciless towards ourselves and not towards others.

Abusive language is a path along which the bridled tongue does not go.

2: Unpermitted conversation – other people's business

It is good and right for us, then, to put off abusive words. And I must next say that the same prohibition applies to unpermitted conversation. There are, dear friends, conversations which are not permitted. Many friends are not conscious of this fact, and I am obliged to instruct myself and others about it. In exposing the question of unpermitted conversation we will research three areas. Firstly we will take the key verses, secondly we will describe the sin in its various facets, and thirdly we will 'examine space and time', that is, where and when this sin is mostly committed.

First of all then, we consider

a. *Key Verses*

The sin of unpermitted conversation is clearly outlined in several verses of sacred Scripture. Let us begin by considering a verse from the Second Epistle to the Thessalonians. In chapter 3 verse 11 we read: 'For we hear that there are some which walk among you disorderly, working not at all, but are busybodies'.

Very many people like the sort of sermon which has nothing to do with their own lives. This is a serious fault. The glory of Christ is in question if we misuse our tongues. The apostle Paul, in the chapter from which we have just quoted, in the sixth verse commands the brethren to do something which sounds really strange in our days of ecumenicity. Paul commands some Christians that they should 'withdraw themselves' from other Christians! These days everybody is talking about unity, but, it seems to me, a unity not based upon biblical principles. The desire of many is unity, no matter how high the cost. The apostle, however, speaks thus: 'Now we command you, brethren, in the name of our Lord Jesus Christ, that ye withdraw yourselves from every brother that walketh disorderly, and not after the tradition which he received of us'.

And the Apostle tells us clearly the nature of this disorderliness. He says: 'working not at all' – Certain Christians were idle, but they thought themselves spiritual because they were waiting for Christ to come. Paul, however, taught: 'If any would not work, neither should he eat'. You must not feed those who are unwilling to work. But not only were they idlers, 'working not at all', but their tongues were actually overworked: 'but are busybodies'.

They refrain from doing what they ought to be doing, but they engage in that which they ought not to be doing. Meddling in other people's business is not permitted in the church of God.

There is a second text which bears on the subject. It is to be found in 1 Timothy 5: 13. In this chapter the apostle is speaking about two kinds of widows. Of the young widows Paul writes: 'And withal they learn to be idle, wandering about from house to house; and not only idle, but tattlers also and busybodies, speaking things which they ought not'. Here we see the same thing as in the verse mentioned previously.

How does Paul describe these widows whom he rebukes? In relation to their tongue he describes them in three words. Firstly 'tattlers', which means that they were full of tales about everything. The second word is 'busybodies'; they were people who meddled in others' affairs, which was a breaking of the law of Christ, and thirdly, 'speaking things which they ought not'. They spoke that which it was not permitted them to speak. And that is why I have entitled this point unpermitted conversation. This has to do with things that Christians have no right to mention. It is none of their business.

Yet another key verse for this theme we find in 1 Peter chapter 4. Here the apostle Peter is writing about Christians who are being persecuted because of their faith in Christ. True Christians have often suffered persecution. But if we undergo it, then it must always be because of our faith alone. It must not be for other reasons, for Scripture says, 'Let none of you suffer as a murderer, or as a thief, or as an evildoer, or *as a busybody in other men's matters*' (1 Peter 4: 15).

Busybodies in other men's matters commit a sin which is linked with murder, theft, and evildoing! That is what the Bible says. Being a busybody is not in harmony with the Christian religion. The Bible says: 'Thou shalt not go up and down as a talebearer among thy people' (Leviticus 19: 16). This refers to persons who went about from tent to tent, bearing tales, and being a busybody in other men's matters. The Bible says: 'A talebearer revealeth secrets: but he that is of a faithful spirit concealeth the matter' (Proverbs 11: 13). The slanderer wanders and roams around. The purpose of this wandering about is to broadcast secrets. He just cannot keep quiet. These are men and women who are always wanting to hear some new thing and spread it around constantly. They are busybodies in other men's matters.

And again, in Proverbs 18: 8, 'The words of a talebearer are as wounds, and they go down into the innermost parts of the belly'. A slanderer, or whisperer, goes about from ear to ear, saying, 'Did you know?', 'Have you heard?', 'Can you guess what's happened?', 'Do you know why?' A whisperer!

Solomon continues further: 'He that goeth about as a talebearer revealeth secrets: therefore meddle not with him that flattereth with his lips' (Proverbs 20: 19). Keeping away from the whisperer, and all those who meddle in other people's business is most of all what is meant in 'therefore meddle not with him that flattereth with his lips'. That is biblical, and in accordance with both the Old and the New Testament.

One more verse: 'Where no wood is, there the fire goeth out: so where there is no talebearer, the strife ceaseth' (Proverbs 26: 20). What happens when there is no wood in a fire? All that is left is white ash. In the same way, where there is no talebearer, the quarrelling stops. But all the while a talebearer is around, or someone who is a busy-body in other men's matters, strife flares up.

b.   *An outline of the sin in its various facets*
How does this sin manifest itself in the congregation of God?

It manifests itself when you find yourselves with someone from the congregation, discussing the problem of a brother who is not present with you, and especially when you are discussing something which that brother would not like to have discussed.

[37]

One of the sinful inclinations of our evil nature is that we want to know about things which are none of our concern or business. As I hinted formerly, it seems to me that these desires are satanic. The desire to know everything about somebody is of the devil. God is omniscient, man is not. Only God has the right to know everything about anybody, man does not.

Beloved, we must not be so inquisitive as to find out more about a brother or sister than he or she thinks good to reveal to us. It is exceedingly sinful to want to intrude into the personal problems of our brethren and sisters. Their personal, domestic affairs are none of our business. How much a person is paid or is not paid is none of our business. Why someone is getting married earlier and someone else is getting married later is not our affair. Why this person has three children, that person has six, and another person has not got any is no concern of ours.

And if a brother is in trouble, let us not make a detailed examination. Love does not wait for details, love helps out. My brother does not need to tell all so that I can pray for him. Whoever asks for details 'so that he can pray' is trying to pry into other men's matters!

For this reason I am against a person's confessing his past to someone else in great detail. It is written: 'Confess your faults one to another and pray one for another that you may be healed. The effectual, fervent prayer of a righteous man availeth much', but be satisfied with what your brother wishes to confide and do not cross-examine him for the details. It is enough that he, or she, should say

[38]

to you, 'I have sinned greatly' and nothing more. In no way must we go into details. That is my attitude towards you, brethren, and this should be the attitude of you all.

We must not pry into the personal affairs of our brother or sister, for that is neither our concern nor our business. Nor should we discuss the affairs of other people which have not been told to us. By no means are we to do that! 'Who art thou that judgest another man's servant'? says the apostle Paul in Romans 14: 4, 'to his own master he standeth or falleth'.

Whence do we get the right to debate our brother's actions? But what if such an action offends me? someone may ask. The Bible is clear on this. 'If thine eye offend thee, pluck it out and cast it from thee'. That is my concern. My business, then, is not to judge others, but rather to discipline myself!

But what if I see that my brother is doing something not in accordance with Scripture? In this case I must not go off and discuss the matter with others, rather, I must do as the Lord Jesus teaches: 'Moreover if thy brother shall trespass against thee, go and tell him his fault between thee and him alone: if he shall hear thee, thou hast gained thy brother' (Matthew 18: 15). Thus you are not to tell tales about him to others but to go to him alone and speak to him alone and with nobody else. Go to him in love and speak to him and show him from Scripture that what he is doing is not good. If he will not hear you, call two more witnesses. If he will not hear them, then tell the church. The Bible is clear about what I must do if my brother trespasses against me (Matthew 18: 15 onwards). In no case do I have the right to discuss him with a third party, for that is not my task. In the Serbo-Croatian language we have a true saying, which goes, 'Whoever accuses another to you is he who will accuse you to another'.

And when a certain brother or sister commits a sin, we must have a biblical basis for its being a sin. But when it is a question of Christian liberty, we had better bind our lips and bridle our tongue.

Let us not put ourselves in the place of God. God has not handed over to us his throne, that we might distinguish what someone can and cannot do. James says well: 'Speak not evil one of another, brethren. He that speaketh evil of his brother, and judgeth his brother, speaketh evil of the law, and judgeth the law: but if thou judge the law, thou art not a doer of the law, but a judge. There is one lawgiver, who is able to save and to destroy: who art thou that judgest another?' (James 4: 11, 12). Do we grasp what James is teaching here? Whoever speaks evil of or judges his brother is playing the role of God, and God does not allow that.

That is why I think that a great sin is committed when men and women are judged by what hair style they have and whether they wear a beard or not, or even by what clothes they wear. If the Bible is silent about something, then we must also be silent. Of course, as a preacher I may say what is best and most fitting, but I must not pronounce judgment on my fellows, because if I start judging I take over what is God's right: a right God gives to no-one.

And so, brothers and sisters, let us make an effort from today onwards not to speak injuriously with others about anybody, or anybody's private life. Otherwise we shall come under judgment as those who are busybodies in other men's matters.

Many people do not have the courage to talk to somebody face to face, but then they speak evil around and about. But we must not talk about the business of others, even in repect of innocent things, unless there is clear need to do so.

c.   *When and where is this sin committed?*

There are idlers who do no work of their own, says Paul, in writing to Timothy. There are young widows who do nothing but wander about from house to house, 'speaking things that they ought not'.

In modern days there are those who drop in for coffee at other women's houses for no apparent reason, and who do no work other than to pry into other people's business. Their coffee is not sweet unless somebody is being condemned over it. The husbands are out at work and the wives are on the prowl. And in those places where life is different from the way it is here, and there are more telephones, the women operate telephonically. By means of the telephone they 'wander from house to house'.

I am not belittling women. To tell you the truth I value women no less than men. But nonetheless I have to say that it is women who are the more inclined to do this sort of thing.

Yet there are reasons for this, especially as regards housewives. To be constantly within four walls is not easy for a woman. They need to get out and see a few friends, to have a good chat with them. And here is where the temptation lies. What are they to chat about? Here is a particular temptation for widows and single women. They miss their friends, which is completely natural. But do take heed not to speak evil of anybody and not to be a busybody in other people's matters! A woman needs to go and see her friend, or chat by telephone, if she has one. However, telling tales about a third party is extremely dangerous.

How I wish I had never known or heard certain things about certain people. The talebearer separates close friends. The talebearer sets up walls between people, splits up brotherhood. These things are of Satan.

The congregation of Christ is a family. We all know something about one another and wish to help one another. We do not come to the congregation as some go to the theatre, going away without any regard for those around them. We are a family. The devil knows this and greatly detests the fact. And he strives to create division. The Bible says that 'when one suffers, others suffer with him, when one rejoices others rejoice with him'. 'Bear one another's burdens and thus fulfil ye the law of Christ'. 'Comfort one another and pray for one another'. But as soon as the devil sees this, he begins to labour to create divisions by means of evil speaking.

Do we see Satan's intentions? If we do see them, here are a few practical lessons.

3: Practical lessons
We purpose to speak about this in the following sermon, but allow me to give you today a few practical lessons for believers, and a few for non-believers.

a. *Lessons for believers*

The apostle Paul writes to the Colossians: 'If ye then be risen with Christ, seek those things which are above, where Christ sitteth on the right hand of God' (Colossians 3: 1). We have passed from death into life. We have within ourselves the life of Christ. And because we have a new life, he continues to say in verse 8: 'But now ye also put off all these; anger, wrath, malice, blasphemy, filthy communication out of your mouth. Lie not one to another, seeing that ye have put off the old man with his deeds; and have put on the new man, which is renewed in knowledge after the image of him that created him: . . . Put on therefore, as the elect of God, holy and beloved, bowels of mercies, kindness, humbleness of mind, meekness, long-suffering; forbearing one another, and forgiving one another . . . And above all these things put on charity, which is the bond of perfectness'.

Here Paul uses two significant words. He says 'put off' and 'put on. 'Put off' means to confess that evil speaking, abusive language, and being a busy-body are sinful, and to repent of these sins. Regardless of sins that one's husband, wife, or others may be committing, a believer must not give place to abusive language. Let us pray to the Lord and ask him to cleanse us from all desire to use it. When the prophet Isaiah saw the holiness of God, he exclaimed: 'Woe is me! for I am undone; because I am a man of unclean lips . . .'.

Only when we forget our own weaknesses do we become self-righteous like the Pharisees, and judge and speak evil of others. But when we put off these things and experience repentance and cleansing, we then go a step further: we dress ourselves. We seek the fulness of the Spirit and of love. Let us pray that the Lord would set a watch on our tongue, and before each and every conversation let us pray for God's guidance. And then, when somebody shows his weaknesses, we shall show longsuffering, gentleness, forgiveness and love.

If we are children of God we will behave in this way, but if we do not, then our coming to meetings is in vain; in vain is our prayer, our singing, our offering, for James says: 'If any man among you seem to be religious, and bridleth not his tongue, but deceiveth his own heart, this man's religion is vain'.

All this is advice for believers for today!

b. *Advice to the unconverted*

To speak generally, those who are unconverted cannot but backbite and slander others. Of course, not all of you are like this, for not all sinners manifest their sin in the same manner. The rich young ruler displayed his sinful nature through cupidity. His possessions controlled his life. The Samaritan woman was a slave to immorality. Some have been slaves to drunkenness. But the majority of sinners combine to express their nature in a wicked, unbridled tongue.

In Matthew 12, the Pharisees accused Christ, saying that all the miracles he worked were done with the help of demoniacal power. They were guilty of the misuse of the tongue. Therefore Jesus told them: 'Either make the tree good, and his fruit good; or else make the tree corrupt, and his fruit corrupt: for the tree is known by his fruit. O generation of vipers, how can ye, being evil, speak good things? for out of the abundance of the heart the mouth speaketh. A good man out of the good treasure of the heart bringeth forth good things: and an evil man out of the evil treasure bringeth forth evil things'. Do you understand this?

A tree is distinguished from other trees by its fruit. That is a visible sign. Therefore the Lord says: 'How can ye, being evil, speak good things? for out of the abundance of the heart the mouth speaketh'. And then he says: 'A good man (a converted man) out of the good treasure of the heart (out of a converted heart) bringeth forth good things (speaks good things): and an evil man (an unconverted man) out of the evil treasure (out of an unconverted heart) bringeth forth evil things (speaks evil things)'. Whispering, backbiting, abusive language, meddling in other people's affairs, these are all fruits of a vile, unconverted heart.

This is why the Lord Jesus said, 'Ye must be born again'. You have to change the tree in order to grow good fruit. From man's old nature no good fruit is to be expected. An entirely new nature must be bestowed by the Spirit of God.

If God has shown you your sin today, you must not run away, but rather turn to Jesus Christ. He is the only One who can save you from your sins. But if you fail to do this, one day you will not be able to escape Judgment, for the Lord Jesus says: 'But I say to you, That every idle word that men shall speak, they shall give account thereof in the day of judgment'.

If you surrender yourself to the Lord and Saviour Jesus Christ, he will give you a new tongue, a tongue which is a spring of life. This speech will strengthen others, comfort them and make them whole. When the fountain is cleansed, the water is clean also.

We need the Lord Jesus to cleanse us with his blood, his Spirit and his Word. This is called salvation, salvation from a rotten heart and corrupt speech. Lips which were the source of putrefaction are now a fountain of blessing. True religion brings this about. But if our words do not bring blessing and life to those round about us, that is a sign that there is no such religion in our hearts.

Jesus died for our sins and has cleansed us from sin. He lives within us, and gives us strength to live according to his will. If we are saved, then we are saved from an unbridled tongue. If we do believe, then we will obey this message of Scripture.

3

A BRIDLE FOR THE TONGUE

*If any man among you seem to be religious, and bridleth
not his tongue, but deceiveth his own heart, this man's
religion is vain.*
(James 1: 26).

On the basis of this verse I am expounding to you
the theme: *A bridled tongue is a measure of true
faith.* Up to now we have studied four ways in
which a bridled tongue is determined not to go.
These four ways, as found in Scripture, I have
chosen because we, as a congregation, need to take
them to heart. In brief, we saw that a bridled
tongue will not go the way of false witness, nor of
corrupt speech. In the same way a bridled tongue
will not follow the path of abusive, shameful
language, nor of backbiting, which is related to
being a busybody in other men's matters. I hope
that God has reminded us that his Word is directed
to us, and that we have repented of our sin before
him, and if necessary we have gone to apologize if
we have offended anyone with our tongue.

Today I wish to conclude this series with two very
practical lessons; first, how can we have a bridled
tongue? second, what sort of bridles must we use
for our tongue and speech? If somebody needs
bridles for a horse or a mule, he goes to the
saddlery and buys them. but where can we obtain a
bridle for our tongue?

I know that some Christians of today do not like
this sort of preaching. They call it moralizing. 'Just

think,' somebody will say, 'today Simo is going to tell us where we can find a bridle for our tongues'! Some people will call us legalists. For this reason I wish, before we start this study, to explain the biblical, evangelical justification for this sort of preaching.

We know, I hope, that the apostles, when they were instructing new converts in a life of godliness, did not solely proclaim great biblical teachings or doctrines, nor did they describe only the glory of the life of Christ as being of exemplary holiness, but they also gave especially detailed instructions concerning the Christian's life of godliness. Here is one example from 1 Thessalonians 4: 1, 2: 'Furthermore then we beseech you, brethren, and exhort you by the Lord Jesus, that as ye have received of us how ye ought to walk and to please God, so ye would abound more and more. For ye know what commandments we gave you by the Lord Jesus'.

The apostles taught believers that they were to please God. And not only this, but also 'how ye ought to walk and to please God'. Read Paul's epistles and see in more detail how old men and old women should walk, how boys and girls, widows, deacons and elders, husbands, wives, children and servants should walk. In 1 Timothy 4: 11 Paul writes to Timothy: 'These things command and teach'. What does he command and teach? Practical and detailed instruction for godly conversation! When we read Titus chapter 2 we find the same thing. Paul instructs Titus to instruct elderly men and women, the young, servants, *etc.,* how they should live. And whoever teaches in this manner is a good servant of Jesus Christ. It is healthy teaching.

[48]

Paul says in 2 Timothy 3: 16, 'All scripture is given by inspiration of God, and is profitable for doctrine, for reproof, for correction, for instruction in righteousness'. According to this, the Bible gives us the right for this type of instructing. It is, by its very nature, Christian teaching, and not moralizing. Our instructing is with a motive very different from moralizing.

When the apostle Paul instructs husbands, wives, children, servants, *etc.*, how they ought to walk, he begins thus: 'Be ye therefore followers of God, as dear children; And walk in love, as Christ also hath loved us, and hath given himself for us an offering and a sacrifice to God for a sweetsmelling savour' (Ephesians 5: 1, 2). All teaching is Christian if it originates from Christ and God. A moralizer teaches, 'Do this, because it is good in and of itself', but Christian morality comes from Christ. Jesus said: 'If ye love me, keep my commandments'.

This is why I have no sympathy for those who call this sort of teaching moralizing. They do not know what moralizing is, nor what Christian holiness is. Paul writes to the Thessalonians to direct them 'how to walk and to please God'. This may sound like moralizing or legalism to the unconverted who do not know the Lord, and to those ministers who want to make themselves wiser than the apostles. But those who do know the Lord have an inward desire to please him.

We know God and Christ, and wish to please him in every detail. It is the unconverted, rebels against God, who are unable to endure this sort of teaching. But enough of that! We, who are here, are not satisfied with futile religion and therefore we are interested in how we might bridle our tongue.

Do you think that God is so harsh as to require of us a bridled tongue without telling us what these bridles are? Thank the Lord that it is not so.

We may say that there are two sorts of material necessary for the production of the bridle: they are, the direct and the indirect.

1: Direct material for the production of the bridle

The direct material for the bridle is threefold: Firstly, persistent prayer; secondly, conscious heed-taking or watchfulness; and thirdly, constant recollection of Scripture.

a. *Persistent prayer*

He who wishes to have a bridled tongue must be persistent in prayer. The key passage of Scripture for this is Psalm 141, written by David.

Above all, my dear friends, the obligation to bridle our tongues is ours. The Lord Jesus will not do this in our stead. James actually says: 'If any man . . . seem to be religious and bridleth not his* tongue . . .'. Therefore it is *our* duty, as converted people, to bridle our tongue. Prayer is involved in this.

In the first two verses of Psalm 141 the Psalmist asks God to accept and help him while he prays: 'Lord, I cry unto thee: make haste unto me; give ear unto my voice, when I cry unto thee. Let my prayer be set forth before thee as incense; and the lifting up of my hands as the evening sacrifice'. He

---

*This is clearer in Serbian where one word for 'his' bears the weight of 'his own'.

prays that the Lord would help him to pray. Do we pray like this?

Thus he indicates to God why he is praying: 'Set a watch, O LORD, before my mouth; keep the door of my lips. Incline not my heart to any evil thing . . .' 'My heart': here he is praying about the state of his heart. After this he asks that God would give him the blessing of being able to endure the reproof of the righteous man gladly. But the first thing in the list he prays for is: 'Set a watch, O LORD, before my mouth; keep the door of my lips'.

David was a soldier. He is expressing himself pictorially here, using images from martial life. A watchman, or sentry, was a soldier who was to be found on the walls, and who took heed lest the enemy came near, or anyone who was not supposed to do so should go outside, such as a prisoner. This picture David uses for the mouth and tongue. He compares the mouth to the gates of the city: 'Set a watch, O LORD, before my mouth; keep the door of my lips'.

I can name the soldiers needed to watch our tongue and lips? There are four of them. They are: Verity, Charity, Necessity and Wisdom. If any word wants to get out of the door of my lips, let it expect to meet these four soldiers on the way.

Verity always asks whether the word to be spoken is true or not. If not, back he goes!

But if it is true, then a second sentry arrives, *Charity* by name, who asks whether the mouth wishes to speak because love demands it. Even if it involves a question of a reproach to somebody, it must be in love. 'Speak the truth in love'. If it does not turn out thus, then soldier Charity does not let it pass.

But if it answers the demands of the first two soldiers, a third watchman, Necessity, appears, who asks: 'Is it really necessary that this should be said'? '*Must* you go outside, or are you just taking a stroll'? 'If you do not go in the name of necessity, turn back'.

But if it is necessary, a fourth look-out arrives, who is called *Wisdom*. Soldier Wisdom asks whether it would not be better if you said this or that a few hours, a few days, or even a few weeks later.

And only if that which we want to say can meet the demands of these four soldiers may we speak. Thus David prays: 'Set a watch, O LORD, before my mouth; keep the door of my lips'.

David saw the need of such a prayer, for he himself was in danger of sinning. David saw his own inability to obey God without divine help, and thus prayed to the Lord. He saw the great importance of a bridled tongue.

In Psalm 19: 13, 14, David prays: 'Keep back thy servant also from presumptuous sins; let them not have dominion over me: then shall I be upright, and I shall be innocent from the great transgression'. This is a general prayer, but after this it becomes specific: 'Let the words of my mouth and the meditation of my heart, be acceptable in thy sight, O Lord, my strength, and my redeemer'.

Perhaps the reason why we have so often lacked a bridled tongue is that we have not prayed persistently for it. I think that the words of James are valid here: 'Ye have not, because ye ask not'.

This needs to be our daily prayer. We meet with people many times a day, and how often do we pray as well as speak? Let us pray regularly that the Lord would set these four watchmen at the doors of our lips, and we shall find that the Lord is willing to help us in all our conversations with others.

b. *Conscious heed-taking*

Prayer and watchfulness go hand in hand. The Lord Jesus told his disciples: 'Watch and pray, that ye enter not into temptation: the spirit indeed is willing, but the flesh is weak' (Matthew 26: 41). Therefore we are to take conscious care whenever we speak. David also says in Psalm 39: 1, 'I said, I will take heed to my ways, that I sin not with my tongue: I will keep my mouth with a bridle, while the wicked is before me'. David is distinguished in that he not only prays, but also takes heed to his ways, especially in speech.

'I will keep my mouth with a bridle'. This teaches me that before I start to speak, I must consider. I will always ask those four watchmen what to say, and how and when.

As for James, in chapter 1: 19 of his epistle, he says: 'Wherefore, my beloved brethren, let every man be swift to hear, slow to speak, slow to wrath'. He means that we are consciously to bridle our tongues. But why? Solomon gives us the answer in Proverbs 10: 19, 'In the multitude of words there wanteth not sin: but he that refraineth his lips is wise'. Whoever speaks without any sentries, who-ever does not take conscious heed, will commit many sins. To use too many words is a sign that the tongue is not bridled, 'but he that refraineth his lips is wise'. You will notice that here it is not the Lord

[53]

who is refraining our lips, but rather it is we who have to refrain them. He who does this is wise.

And again, in Proverbs 17: 27, Solomon says: 'He that hath knowledge spareth his words: and a man of understanding is of an excellent spirit'. God indicates that it is well if we are miserly with our words. So imagine that for every wrong word we speak we must pay £10. How very quickly would we collapse into destitution!

I urge you to believe that whenever we speak and our words do not correspond to the demands of those four sentries we lose much. And whenever we speak in accordance with their demands we gain much blessing. Therefore let us keep to God's rules, dear brothers and sisters; let us heed his instructions, for life and death is in the power of the tongue.

Let me remind you how unpleasant it is when someone eats garlic and then goes out among friends for a chat. And when we sense that we are being found unpleasant we no longer feel like speaking. Some people ought to eat garlic all the time just to learn how to keep quiet! And how much more upsetting it is when somebody speaks without weighing his words! So let us economize on our words. When we speak to people let us say only what is desirable and necessary. Let us be slow to speak. But when we perceive that the conversation is beginning to turn in a wrong direction, let us check it. Let us issue a warning!

c. *The constant recollection of God's warnings*
Why are there so many warnings for Christians in the Bible? We know why they are there for non-believers. God does not want them to go to hell.

God does not wish that you should go to hell and so he trips you up on the way there. But why are there warnings on the believer's path? The believer is not travelling to hell but to heaven. He is walking the narrow way. These warnings are not like the rocks on the broad way to save men from hell, rather they are signposts on the narrow way that leads to heaven!

Signposts! At every bend, at every turn of the narrow way, there are signs which show us where a saved man does not go. The warnings are the means which keep the true believer on the narrow road to heaven. Whoever takes no notice of the warnings and does not care about them displays by this the dreadful condition of his soul. It is the unsaved who are careless.

Here are some warnings.

In Proverbs 13: 3, 'He that keepeth his mouth keepeth his life: but he that openeth wide his lips shall have destruction'. Thus it is important to have bridles. He that openeth wide his lips shall have destruction. If we are believers, and we yield on this point, we come to grief as well. Beloved in the Lord, God warns us not to sin. If we have the life of Christ we will gladly listen to this warning for our own good. Indeed, we must constantly think about this warning.

In Psalm 101: 5 the psalmist says: 'Whoso privily slandereth his neighbour, him will I cut off: him that hath an high look and a proud heart will I not suffer'. God cuts off the slanderer! The believer will not walk this way.

Brothers and sisters, whenever we have to speak and discuss something, we should pray. Prayer helps greatly. These are the direct bridles: persistent prayer, conscious watchfulness, and constant recollection of God's warnings. This is to exercise oneself in godliness, it is to pluck out my eye and cut off my hand if they offend me. It is in this that true religion consists.

2: Indirect material

Up to now we have been speaking about direct material for the bridling of the tongue. Now we shall speak about the indirect. However, it goes without saying that only those who are saved desire and strive to please their Saviour, especially in their speech. The indirect material is as follows:

a. *To be filled with the Spirit*

The apostle Paul writes to the Ephesians: 'And be not drunk with wine, wherein is excess; but be filled with the Spirit'. What does this mean, 'be filled with the Spirit'? It is not difficult to answer the question. Actually, a man who is filled with the Spirit is under the control of the Holy Spirit, not under the control of wine. And whether a man is under the control of the Holy Spirit or under the influence of wine can be seen with the utmost clearness in his speech! Thus the apostle resumes: 'Speaking to yourselves . . .'; therefore, his exhortation has to do with the tongue. What does a Spirit-controlled tongue speak? 'Speaking to yourselves in psalms and hymns and spiritual songs, singing and making melody in your heart to the Lord; giving thanks always for all things unto God and the Father in the name of our Lord Jesus Christ; submitting yourselves one to another in the fear of God' (Ephesians 5: 18 onwards).

This is a description of a healthy spiritual condition, which inevitably manifests itself in speech. We no longer want to slander one another or abuse one another. We do not meddle in that which does not concern us, but rather 'submit ourselves one to another in the fear of God'. A man's speech shows whether he has the fulness of the Spirit.

Comparable verses to these are to be found in the third chapter of Colossians. There Paul says that believers are 'risen with Christ'. In the 5th verse he commands that we should mortify our members, and in verses 8 and 9 that we should put off the old man and put on the new. And then in the 16th verse he says: 'Let the word of Christ dwell in you richly in all wisdom; teaching and admonishing one another in psalms and hymns and spiritual songs, singing with grace in your hearts to the Lord'.

No-one can get dressed if he has not previously got undressed. One must put off the old in order to put on the new. And nobody will put off the old man if he does not see what sin is. That is why we have spoken earlier about the many sins of the tongue. We must repent, and put off the old ways. But not only that, we must also put on something. And the apostle says what that means. Our clothing is holiness, lovingkindness, bowels of mercies, goodness, humbleness, meekness, longsuffering, forbearance and instruction. And whoever is clothed in these virtues will not speak abusively and corruptly, nor be a busybody in other men's matters. Whoever wishes to have a bridled tongue must pay attention to his spiritual health.

Let us look at two more passages of Holy

Scripture which will help us to maintain good spiritual health.

'Keep thy heart with all diligence', we read in Proverbs 4: 23, 24, 'for out of it are the issues of life. Put away from thee a froward mouth, and perverse lips put far from thee'. Whoever looks after his heart – his spiritual health – will look after his lips.

The second text is from the words of our Lord in Luke 6: 43–45: 'For a good tree bringeth not forth corrupt fruit; neither doth a corrupt tree bring forth good fruit. For every tree is known by his own fruit. For of thorns men do not gather figs, nor of a bramble bush gather they grapes. A good man out of the good treasure of his heart bringeth forth that which is good; and an evil man out of the evil treasure of his heart bringeth forth that which is evil: for of the abundance of the heart his mouth speaketh'. If the heart is right, the speech will be right also. Evil speech is a sign of an unconverted heart.

Particularly significant are Christ's words: 'of the abundance of the heart his mouth speaketh'. If, then, one's spiritual state is good, one's speech will be good also. In order for the speech to be in order, the spiritual condition must be attended to. Whoever wishes to watch out against all sin must look after his heart. If we start sinning with our tongue, we have a sign that our spiritual health is poor.

b.   *Choosing one's friends carefully*
The second indirect means to the bridling of the tongue is the careful choosing of one's friendships. The Bible says: 'He that walketh with wise men shall be wise: but a companion of fools shall be destroyed' (Proverbs 13: 20). I must only remind

you that fools in the biblical sense are not the intellectually dull, but those who are public sinners. The people with whom you mix show what sort of person you are.

Therefore we find in the Bible commands that we should pay attention to good examples and follow them, and keep aloof from bad examples. How important this is in speech! Solomon says: 'He that goeth about as a talebearer revealeth secrets: therefore meddle not with him that flattereth with his lips' (Proverbs 20: 19). Do not mix with those that flatter with their lips.

In the same manner as the Lord says: 'Thou shalt have no other gods before me', 'Thou shalt not kill', 'Thou shalt not commit adultery', he also teaches us not to make friends with those who have an unbridled tongue.

And in 2 Thessalonians 3: 6–11 the apostle Paul commands that we withdraw ourselves from every brother who has an unbridled tongue and is a busybody. It is right to separate from everybody who meddles in other people's affairs. But if we fail to do this, we shall also become such as they. For this reason we dare not mix with careless walkers, rather we must make friends with such as are exemplary. In Philippians 3: 17, the apostle Paul writes: 'Brethren, be followers together of me, and mark them which walk so as ye have us for an ensample'. Make sure that your friendships are with only those who have a bridled tongue.

Whom ought we to please, God or men? When we separate ourselves, somebody will indeed be displeased, but it is right to withdraw from those who do us no good. If someone's friendship is not making us better, but worse, we had better avoid that friendship. Let us withdraw ourselves from those who bear all sorts of tales on their tongues.

In this manner we shall help both ourselves and those from whom we withdraw. Ourselves, because we are keeping from sin, and those who are sinning, in that they might be put to shame and walk more closely with the Lord. Love does this. Love desires the good of the sinner. This is very necessary for some. Let us be friends with those who help us to be like Christ.

c. *Public reproof to those who are sinning*

To rebuke sin falls into the category of indirect material for the bridle. 'Reprove not a scorner, lest he hate thee: rebuke a wise man and he will love thee' (Proverbs 9: 8).

Wise Solomon calls the man a scorner who does not appreciate a loving rebuke. But one who accepts reproof is wise and faithful. If you rebuke a humble believer he will love you because you have reproved him.

Solomon also says in Proverbs 13: 18, 'Poverty and shame shall be to him that refuseth instruction: but he that regardeth reproof shall be honoured'. In 15: 31, 32 we read, 'The ear that heareth the reproof of life abideth among the wise. He that refuseth instruction despiseth his own soul: but he that heareth reproof getteth understanding'. Again in Proverbs 6: 23, 'For the commandment is a lamp; and the law is light; and reproofs of instruction are the way of life'.

When God saves a person, he places him on the narrow way and keeps him to the end. And reproof is one of the means by which God keeps him in the way. 'Reproofs of instruction are the way of life'.

'He that refuseth reproof erreth' says Solomon in Proverbs 10: 17. He who cannot bear reproach, who 'refuseth reproof', will surely lose his way. A traveller who has mistaken his route and cannot tolerate being shown the correct way must be lost indeed. It is by a similar stubbornness that multitudes miss the way of life. In 12: 1, 'he that hateth reproof is brutish'; in 15: 10, 'Correction is grievous unto him that forsaketh the way: and he that hateth reproof shall die'. In Hebrews we read: 'Take heed, brethren, lest there be in any of you an evil heart of unbelief, in departing from the living God' (3: 12).

Because talking has to do with friendship, we are liable to sin most of all when we are with someone who is a friend. Thus rebuke here is extremely profitable. As a minister of the gospel I have the right to preach about this and to reprove publicly. And the wise will understand and accept it. Here Solomon's words are valid: 'Open rebuke is better than secret love. Faithful are the wounds of a friend; but the kisses of an enemy are deceitful' (27: 5, 6). It is good for us that our friends should rebuke us and show us our mistakes, although for the moment these reproofs seem like blows, and are as painful as wounds. But rebukes are necessary, and whoever loves another will reprove him if he finds him yielding to sin. Let us display our love when we hear that somebody is not bridling his tongue! Our ears must not be as rubbish bins for false witness, evil tales, abusive language and meddlings in others' business. For what enters the ears enters the heart. 'Open rebuke is better than secret love'.

'For whom the Lord loveth he chasteneth, and scourgeth every son whom he receiveth' (Hebrews 12: 6). It is in full accordance with love that a father applies the rod to his son now and again. But of course it is unavailing for a father to beat his children without showing love in other things. Our heavenly Father shows us his love in thousands of positive ways, including the use of chastisement. Whoever loves you will show that love in other things and you will not become irritable if he also rebukes you. 'As many as I love, I rebuke and chasten: be zealous therefore and repent', said the Lord to the church of Laodicea (Rev. 3: 19).

When we rebuke along biblical lines, in love, we, in doing so, help to heal one another. It goes without saying that our motive is important. On it depends whether we shall be a help or a hindrance.

Therefore brothers and sisters, let us use these means to the bridling of our tongue. There are three direct means; persistent prayer, conscious watchfulness in our speech, and constant recollection of God's warnings. Also we have three indirect means – attending to our spiritual condition (fulness of the Spirit), careful choosing of our friendships, and reproving.

Let us pay attention, brethren, to our tongue.

May the Lord help us to avoid vain religion! Now nobody can accuse me of not having instructed you as to how we might have a bridled tongue. And may the Lord help us all, not to be hearers only, but also doers of the Word.

Lord, add thy blessing. Amen.